T0149698

WHICH?

Matumayini Lilia
Mboleza

BALBOA.PRESS

A DIVISION OF HAY HOUSE

Balboa Press books may be ordered through booksellers or by contacting:

Balboa Press
A Division of Hay House
1663 Liberty Drive
Bloomington, IN 47403
www.balboapress.com.au
1 (877) 407-4847

Because of the dynamic nature of the Internet, any web addresses or links contained in this book may have changed since publication and may no longer be valid. The views expressed in this work are solely those of the author and do not necessarily reflect the views of the publisher, and the publisher hereby disclaims any responsibility for them.

The author of this book does not dispense medical advice or prescribe the use of any technique as a form of treatment for physical, emotional, or medical problems without the advice of a physician, either directly or indirectly. The intent of the author is only to offer information of a general nature to help you in your quest for emotional and spiritual well-being. In the event you use any of the information in this book for yourself, which is your constitutional right, the author and the publisher assume no responsibility for your actions.

Any people depicted in stock imagery provided by Getty Images are models, and such images are being used for illustrative purposes only. Certain stock imagery © Getty Images.

Print information available on the last page.

ISBN: 978-1-5043-2070-2 (sc)
ISBN: 978-1-5043-2071-9 (e)

Balboa Press rev. date: 02/07/2020

Introduction

The word which is pronoun · determiner. Determiner: "which."
The word, "which," means asking for information specifying
one or more people or things from a definite set. For example:
"which are the best varieties of grapes for long keeping? "Which
is pronoun · determiner. Pronoun: "which. "The word, "which,"
means, used referring to something previously mentioned when
introducing a clause giving further information. For example: "a
conference in Vienna which ended on Friday."

Questions you should ask yourself or somebody daily

DEFINITELY AND HONESTLY, YOU MUST GIVE YOURSELF A CHANCE TO DO, SOME SELF-STUDY, THROUGH THESE ENGLISH LANGUAGE AND VOCABULARY IMPROVEMENTS. YOU MUST ALWAYS BE AWARE OF WHAT YOU SPEAK EACH DAYS OF YOUR LIFE; AS THE FOLLOWING:

- RULE NUMBER ONE, "YOU MUST ALWAYS KNOW HOW TO PRONOUNCIATE ALL THE WORDS VERY GOOD, THAT ARE FOUND INSIDE EACH QUESTION AS WRITTEN BELOW."

- RULE NUMBER TWO YOU MUST ALWAYS KNOW AND MAKE SURE THAT YOU UNDERSTAND OF HOW TO SPELL EACH SINGLE ENGLISH WORD, "WHICH," ARE FOUND IN ANY PARTICULAR ENGLISH DICTIONARIES.

- RULE NUMBER THREE YOU MUST ALWAYS GAIN AS MUCH UNDERSTAINGS AS POSSIBLE AS YOU CAN OR COULD OR WILL OR WOULD TO BE ABLE TO HELP YOURSELF OR YOUR FAMILY OR FRIEND- FAMILIES OF SOMEWHERE ELSE FROM WHERE YOU LIVE ENGLISH, "APPLICATION FORMS FILL IN." IT IS MUCH IMPORTANT FOR YOU TO HAVE MUCH EXPERIENCES, OF EXPERIENCING ON HOW TO FILL IN AN ENGLISH APPLICATION FORMS.

- RULE NUMBER FOUR BY BOOK READINGS OF, "WHICH?" BOOK WOULD GAIN MUCH KNOWLEDGE OF ENGLISH LANGUAGE VOCABULARY IMPROVEMENT.

SO, PLEASE YOU MUST REMEMBER THAT EVERYTHINGS WHICH
IS WRITTEN INSIDE OF THIS BOOK. YOU MUST NORMALLY OR
USUALLY PUT THIS, "WHICH," BOOK INTO PRACTICE THROUGH
YOUR OWN PERIOD OF TIMES, OF THE EACH YEAR OF YOUR LIFE,
WHETHER YOUR NEGATIVE {BAD} LIFE OR YOUR POSITIVE {GOOD}
LIFE WHICH IS FOUND HERE ON THE EARTH PLANET OR UNIVERSE,
WHERE YOU LIVE.

WHICH IS ABLE?

WHICH IS ACCEPT?

WHICH IS ACCEPTANCE?

WHICH IS ACCEPTABLE?

WHICH IS ACCEPTED?

WHICH IS ACCEPTING?

WHICH IS ACTION?

WHICH IS ACTIVATE?

WHICH IS ACTIVE?

WHICH IS ADD?

WHICH IS ADDITION?

WHICH IS ADORABLE?

WHICH IS ADVANTAGE?

WHICH IS AFFIRM?

WHICH IS AGELESS?

WHICH IS AGREE?

WHICH IS AGREEABLE?

WHICH IS AID?

WHICH IS AIM?

WHICH IS ABUNDANCE?

WHICH IS ACCOUNTABILITY?

WHICH IS ACCOMPLISHMENT?

WHICH IS ACCOMPLISH?

WHICH IS ACCURACY?

WHICH IS ACHIEVEMENT?

WHICH IS WHICH IS ACHIEVE?

WHICH IS ACKNOWLEDGEMENT?

WHICH IS ADAPTABILITY?

WHICH IS ADVENTURE?

WHICH IS ADVENTUROUS?

WHICH IS AGILITY?

WHICH IS ALERTNESS?

WHICH IS AMBITION?

WHICH IS ANTICIPATION?

WHICH IS APPRECIATE?

WHICH IS APPRECIATION

WHICH IS APPRECIATIVE?

WHICH IS APPRECIATIVENESS?

WHICH IS ASSERTIVENESS?

WHICH IS ASSERTIVE?

WHICH IS ATTENTIVENESS?

WHICH IS AUDACITY?

WHICH IS AWARE?

WHICH IS AWARENESS?

WHICH IS AUTHENTIC?

WHICH IS AUTHENTICITY?

WHICH IS ABRACADABRA?

WHICH IS ATTRACTION?

WHICH IS ALLOW?

WHICH IS ALLOWING?

WHICH IS AFFECTION?

WHICH IS AFFECTIONATE?

WHICH IS ABSORBED?

WHICH IS ALERT?

WHICH IS AMAZED?

WHICH IS AWE?

WHICH IS AWED?

WHICH IS ANIMATE?

WHICH IS ANIMATED?

WHICH IS ANIMATING?

WHICH IS ANIMATION?

WHICH IS ANIMATENESS?

WHICH IS ARDENT?

WHICH IS AMAZING?

WHICH IS AWESOME?

WHICH IS AWESOMENESS?

WHICH IS AROUSED?

WHICH IS ASTONISHED?

WHICH IS ASTONISHING?

WHICH IS AMUSED?

WHICH IS AIR?

WHICH IS AIRNESS?

WHICH IS ALOHA?

WHICH IS ADORE?

WHICH IS ADMIRE?

WHICH IS ADMIRABLE?

Matumayini Lilia Mboleza

WHICH IS ALLURE?

WHICH IS ANGEL?

WHICH IS ANGELIC?

WHICH IS ALTRUISM?

WHICH IS ALTRUISTIC?

WHICH IS ABOUND?

WHICH IS ABOUNDING?

WHICH IS ABOUNDS?

WHICH IS ABUNDANT?

WHICH IS ABSOLUTE?

WHICH IS ABSOLUTELY?

WHICH IS ACCESSIBLE?

WHICH IS ACCLAIMED?

WHICH IS ACCOMMODATE?

WHICH IS ACCOMMODATED?

WHICH IS ACCOMMODATION?

WHICH IS ACCOMMODATING?

WHICH IS AMPLE?

WHICH IS APPRECIATIVE JOY?

WHICH IS AMIN?

WHICH IS ACCENTUACTIVITY?

WHICH IS ACTABILITY?

WHICH IS AFFABLE?

WHICH IS ALACRITY?

WHICH IS ALTRUCAUSE?

WHICH IS AMIABLE?

WHICH IS ASTOUNDING?

WHICH IS ATTRACTIVE?

WHICH IS ALIVE?

WHICH IS ALIVENESS?

WHICH IS ACCLAIM?

WHICH IS ABUNDANT GRATIFICATION?

WHICH IS ACCLAMATION?

WHICH IS ACCOMPLISHED?

WHICH IS ACCOMPLISHMENTS?

WHICH IS ACCURATE?

WHICH IS ACCURATELY?

WHICH IS ACHIEVABLE,

WHICH IS ACHIEVEMENTS,

WHICH IS ACTION FOR HAPPINESS,

WHICH IS ACTIVE AND CONSTRUCTIVE STEPS?

WHICH IS ACTS OF KINDNESS?

WHICH IS ADAPTABLE?

WHICH IS ADAPTIVE?

WHICH IS ADEQUATE?

WHICH IS ADMIRABLY?

WHICH IS ADMIRATION?

WHICH IS ADMIRED?

WHICH IS ADORED?

WHICH IS ADORING?

WHICH IS ADORINGLY?

WHICH IS ADVANCED?

WHICH IS ADVANTAGEOUS?

WHICH IS ADVANTAGEOUSLY?

WHICH IS ADVANTAGES?

WHICH IS AFFABILITY?

WHICH IS AFFABLY?

WHICH IS AFFINITY?

WHICH IS AFFIRMATION?

WHICH IS AFFIRMATIVE?

WHICH IS AFFLUENCE?

WHICH IS AFFLUENT?

WHICH IS AFFORD?

WHICH IS AFFORDABLE?

WHICH IS AFFORDABLY?

WHICH IS AGILE?

WHICH IS AGILELY?

WHICH IS AGREEABLENESS?

WHICH IS AGREEABLY?

WHICH IS ALIGNED?

WHICH IS ALL IS WELL?

WHICH IS ALLURING?

WHICH IS ALLURINGLY?

WHICH IS ALTERNATIVE HEALING?

WHICH IS ALTRUISTICALLY?

WHICH IS AMAZE?

WHICH IS AMAZEMENT?

WHICH IS AMAZES?

WHICH IS AMAZINGLY?

WHICH IS AMIABILITY?

WHICH IS AMICABILITY?

WHICH IS AMICABLE?

WHICH IS AMICABLY?

WHICH IS AMUSING?

WHICH IS APPEAL?

WHICH IS APPEALING?

WHICH IS APPLAUD?

WHICH IS APPRECIABLE?

WHICH IS APPRECIATED?

WHICH IS APPRECIATES?

WHICH IS APPRECIATION OF BEAUTY?

WHICH IS APPRECIATIVELY?

WHICH IS APPROPRIATE?

WHICH IS APPROVAL?

WHICH IS APPROVE?

WHICH IS ARDOR?

WHICH IS ART OF APPRECIATION?

WHICH IS ART OF STILLNESS?

WHICH IS ART OF WELL-BEING?

WHICH IS ASSURANCE?

WHICH IS A REASON FOR BEING?

WHICH IS ACARONAR?

WHICH IS ACCOMMODATIVE?

WHICH IS ALTITUDINARIAN?

WHICH IS AMAZING WORDS?

WHICH IS AMIABLY?

WHICH IS ACCOLADE?

WHICH IS ACUMEN?

WHICH IS ADJUSTABLE?

WHICH IS ADMIRER?

WHICH IS ADMIRING?

WHICH IS ADMIRINGLY?

WHICH IS ADORER?

WHICH IS ADROIT?

WHICH IS ADROITLY?

WHICH IS ADULATED?

WHICH IS ADULATION?

WHICH IS ADULATORY?

WHICH IS ADVENTURESOME?

WHICH IS ADVOCATED?

WHICH IS AMBITIOUS?

WHICH IS AMBITIOUSLY?

WHICH IS AMELIORATE?

WHICH IS AMENITY?

WHICH IS AMITY?

WHICH IS AMPLY?

WHICH IS AMUSE?

WHICH IS AMUSINGLY?

WHICH IS APOTHEOSIS?

WHICH IS ASSUME YOUR OWN VALUE?

WHICH IS ASTONISHINGLY?

WHICH IS ASTONISHMENT? ATTRIBUTIONAL STYLE
QUESTIONNAIRE (ASQ)?

WHICH IS AUTHENTIC HAPPINESS?

WHICH IS AWAKEN?

WHICH IS AWAKENING?

WHICH IS AWE-GASMIC?

WHICH IS AKASHIC RECORDS?

WHICH IS AURORA?

WHICH IS BEATIFY?

WHICH IS BEATITUDE?

WHICH IS BENEFICIAL?

WHICH IS BENEFIT?

WHICH IS BENEVOLENT?

WHICH IS BELOVED?

WHICH IS BEST?

WHICH IS BETTER?

WHICH IS BLESS?

WHICH IS BLESSING?

WHICH IS BLESSED?

WHICH IS BLISS?

WHICH IS BLISSFULNESS?

WHICH IS BLISSFUL?

WHICH IS BLOOM?

WHICH IS BLOSSOM?

WHICH IS BALANCE?

WHICH IS BALANCED?

WHICH IS BEAUTY?

WHICH IS BEAUTIFUL?

WHICH IS BEAUTIFULLY?

WHICH IS BELONG?

WHICH IS BELONGING?

WHICH IS BOLDNESS?

WHICH IS BRAVERY?

WHICH IS BRILLIANCE?

WHICH IS BRILLIANT?

WHICH IS BLISS ON TAP?

WHICH IS BEYOND FABULOUS?

WHICH IS BIOPHILIA?

WHICH IS BRIGHT?

WHICH IS BRIGHTEN?

WHICH IS BRIGHTNESS?

WHICH IS BALISTIC?

WHICH IS BLASTING?

WHICH IS BLAZING?

WHICH IS BLINDING?

WHICH IS BREATHTAKING?

WHICH IS BUBBLING?

WHICH IS BUSTING?

WHICH IS BLISSCIPLINE?

WHICH IS BUYANCY?

WHICH IS BULLISHNESS?

WHICH IS BRISKNESS?

WHICH IS BUOYANCY?

WHICH IS BREEZINESS?

WHICH IS BRIO?

WHICH IS BE EXTRAORDINARY?

WHICH IS BE HAPPY?

WHICH IS BEAUTIFY?

WHICH IS BEING AT REST?

WHICH IS BENEFACTOR?

WHICH IS BENEFITS?

WHICH IS BENEVOLENCE?

WHICH IS BENEVOLENTLY?

WHICH IS BENEVOLENTLY CHEERFUL STATE OF MIND?

WHICH IS BEST OF ALL POSSIBLE WORLDS?

WHICH IS BEYOND?

WHICH IS BEAUTY IN ALL THINGS?

WHICH IS BEINGNESS?

WHICH IS BELIEVABLE?

WHICH IS BLOOD-BROTHERS?

WHICH IS BOHEMIAN SOUL?

WHICH IS BOHO-SOUL?

WHICH IS BADASSERY?

WHICH IS BEST-SELLING?

WHICH IS BETTER AND BETTER?

WHICH IS BETTER-KNOWN?

WHICH IS BETTER-THAN-EXPECTED?

WHICH IS BEYOND THANK YOU?

WHICH IS BIG VISION?

WHICH IS BLITHESOME?

WHICH IS BLOSSOMING?

WHICH IS BONUS?

WHICH IS BLING BLING?

WHICH IS BUDO?

WHICH IS BLASTING LOVE?

WHICH IS BUDDHAHOOD?

WHICH IS CARE?

WHICH IS CARING?

WHICH IS CALM?

WHICH IS CREATE?

WHICH IS CREATIVE?

WHICH IS CREATIVITY?

WHICH IS CREATIVENESS?

WHICH IS CAPABLE?

WHICH IS CAPABILITY?

WHICH IS CAPABLY?

WHICH IS CELEBRATE?

WHICH IS CELEBRATION?

WHICH IS CERTAIN?

WHICH IS CERTAINTY?

WHICH IS CHARITABLE?

WHICH IS CHARITY?

WHICH IS CHARM?

WHICH IS CHARMING?

WHICH IS CHARMER?

WHICH IS CHOICE?

WHICH IS CLEAN?

WHICH IS CLEANLINESS?

WHICH IS COMFORT?

WHICH IS COMFORTABLE?

WHICH IS COMFORTING?

WHICH IS CUDDLE?

WHICH IS CUDDLING?

WHICH IS CANDOR?

WHICH IS CAREFULNESS?

WHICH IS CHALLENGE?

WHICH IS CHANGE?

WHICH IS CHEERFUL?

WHICH IS CHEERFULNESS?

WHICH IS CLARITY?

WHICH IS COLLABORATION?

WHICH IS COMMITMENT?

WHICH IS COMMUNICATION?

WHICH IS COMMUNITY?

WHICH IS COMPASSION?

WHICH IS COMPASSIONATE?

WHICH IS COMPETENT?

WHICH IS COMPETENCE?

WHICH IS COMPETENCY?

WHICH IS CONCENTRATION?

WHICH IS CONFIDENT?

WHICH IS CONFIDENCE?

WHICH IS CONSCIOUSNESS?

WHICH IS CONSISTENCY?

WHICH IS CONSISTENT?

WHICH IS CONTENT?

WHICH IS CONTENTMENT?

WHICH IS CONTINUITY?

WHICH IS CONTINUOUS?

WHICH IS CONTRIBUTION?

WHICH IS CONVICTION?

WHICH IS CONVINCING?

WHICH IS COOPERATION?

WHICH IS COURAGE?

WHICH IS COURTESY?

WHICH IS COURTEOUS?

WHICH IS CURIOUS?

WHICH IS CURIOSITY?

WHICH IS CHAKRA?

WHICH IS COOL?

WHICH IS CLEAR HEADED?

WHICH IS CENTERED?

WHICH IS CLOSENESS?

WHICH IS COMPANIONSHIP?

WHICH IS CONSIDERATE?

WHICH IS CONSIDERATION?

WHICH IS COMMUNION?

WHICH IS CONNECT?

WHICH IS CONNECTED?

WHICH IS CONNECTION?

WHICH IS CONNECTEDNESS?

WHICH IS CONQUER?

WHICH IS CUTE?

WHICH IS CHARISMA?

WHICH IS CHARISMATIC?

WHICH IS COLLECTED?

WHICH IS CHEERFUL WILLINGNESS?

WHICH IS CHEERS?

WHICH IS CONGRUENCE?

WHICH IS CORDIAL?

WHICH IS CRANK (UP) ?

WHICH IS CAPITAL?

WHICH IS CORKING?

WHICH IS CLEAR?

WHICH IS CARESS?

WHICH IS CHEERFUL MOOD?

WHICH IS COMPLIMENTARY WORDS?

WHICH IS CONTENTED?

WHICH IS COZINESS?

WHICH IS CUTENESS?

WHICH IS CAREFREENESS?

WHICH IS CAREFREE?

WHICH IS CENTERING?

WHICH IS CENTERING MEDITATION?

WHICH IS CITIZEN OF MASTERY?

WHICH IS CO-CREATING?

WHICH IS CO-CREATOR?

WHICH IS COHESION?

WHICH IS CONTINUAL STREAM OF SYNCHRONICITY?

WHICH IS CREATIVE PROCESS?

WHICH IS CREATIVE AFFIRMATIONS?

WHICH IS COMPOSTURE?

WHICH IS CONCORD?

WHICH IS CEREBRO?

WHICH IS CONSCIOUSNESS ENGINEERING?

WHICH IS CHI?

WHICH IS CLASSY?

WHICH IS COPACABANA?

WHICH IS COSMIC AWARENESS?

WHICH IS DIRECTION?

WHICH IS DELICATE?

WHICH IS DECENT?

WHICH IS DESIRABLE?

WHICH IS DELICIOUS?

WHICH IS DELICIOUSNESS?

WHICH IS DO?

WHICH IS DREAM?

WHICH IS DREAMY?

WHICH IS DYNAMIC?

WHICH IS DARING?

WHICH IS DECISIVENESS?

WHICH IS DELIGHT?

WHICH IS DELIGHTED?

WHICH IS DELIGHTFUL?

WHICH IS DEPENDABILITY?

WHICH IS DESIRE?

WHICH IS DETERMINATION?

WHICH IS DEVOTION?

WHICH IS DIGNITY?

WHICH IS DILIGENCE?

WHICH IS DISCIPLINE?

WHICH IS DISCOVERY?

WHICH IS DISCRETION?

WHICH IS DIVERSITY?

WHICH IS DRIVE?

WHICH IS DUTY?

WHICH IS DIVINE?

WHICH IS DAZZLED?

WHICH IS DISNEY?

WHICH IS DEVOTED?

WHICH IS DANDY?

WHICH IS DAIMON?

WHICH IS DEBONAIR?

WHICH IS DETACHMENT?

WHICH IS DEDICATED?

WHICH IS DAUWTRAPPEN?

WHICH IS DAZZLE?

WHICH IS DELIGHTFULLY?

WHICH IS DEFENCELESSNESS?

WHICH IS DEEPER PART OF YOU?

WHICH IS DESERVE?

WHICH IS DESERVEDNESS?

WHICH IS DESERVINGNESS?

WHICH IS DIS-IDENTIFY?

WHICH IS DOPE?

WHICH IS DOPE CHILL OUT?

WHICH IS EMPATHY?

WHICH IS EMPATHIZE?

WHICH IS EMPHATIC?

WHICH IS WHICH IS EASY?

WHICH IS EASILY?

WHICH IS EASIER?

WHICH IS EDUCATE?

WHICH IS EDUCATION?

WHICH IS EDUCATED?

WHICH IS EFFICIENT?

WHICH IS ENABLE?

WHICH IS ENABLED?

WHICH IS ENERGETIC?

WHICH IS ENERGIZE?

WHICH IS ENERGY?

WHICH IS ENGAGE?

WHICH IS ENGAGING?

WHICH IS ENGAGED?

WHICH IS ENJOY?

WHICH IS ENJOYMENT?

WHICH IS ENOUGH?

WHICH IS EAGER?

WHICH IS EAGERNESS?

WHICH IS EFFECTIVENESS?

WHICH IS EFFICIENCY?

WHICH IS ELATION?

WHICH IS ELEGANCE?

WHICH IS ENCOURAGE?

WHICH IS ENCOURAGEMENT?

WHICH IS ENCOURAGED?

WHICH IS ENDURANCE?

WHICH IS EQUALITY?

WHICH IS EXCELLENCE?

WHICH IS EXCELLENT?

WHICH IS EXCITE?

WHICH IS EXCITEMENT?

WHICH IS EXCITED?

WHICH IS EXPERIENCE?

WHICH IS EXPERTISE?

WHICH IS EXPLORATION?

WHICH IS EXPRESSIVENESS?

WHICH IS EXPRESSING?

WHICH IS ENLIGHTENMENT?

WHICH IS ENLIGHTENED?

WHICH IS ETERNAL?

WHICH IS EXALTATION?

WHICH IS EMULATE?

WHICH IS EMPOWER?

WHICH IS EMPOWERING?

WHICH IS EMPOWERED?

WHICH IS EXPANSIVE?

WHICH IS EXHILARATING?

WHICH IS ENTHUSIASTIC?

WHICH IS ENTHUSIASM?

WHICH IS ENGROSSED?

WHICH IS ENCHANTED?

WHICH IS ENTRANCED?

WHICH IS ECSTATIC?

WHICH IS ELATED?

WHICH IS ENTHRALLED?

WHICH IS EXUBERANT?

WHICH IS EXUBERANCE?

WHICH IS EXPECTANT?

WHICH IS EQUANIMOUS?

WHICH IS ENLIVENED?

WHICH IS EFFICACY?

WHICH IS EASE?

WHICH IS EXEMPLARY?

WHICH IS EXTRAORDINARY?

WHICH IS EARNEST?

WHICH IS ELEVATE?

WHICH IS ELEVATED?

WHICH IS EQUANIMITY?

WHICH IS EASE-OF-MIND?

WHICH IS EXCITED ANTICIPATION?

WHICH IS EXTRA?

WHICH IS EQUITY?

WHICH IS EQUITABLY?

WHICH IS EQUITABLE?

WHICH IS EASY TO TALK TO?

WHICH IS EASY TO APPROACH?

WHICH IS ECSTATIFY?

WHICH IS EUDAEMONISM?

WHICH IS EUDAEMONIST?

WHICH IS EUDAEMONISTIC?

WHICH IS EUDAIMONIA?

WHICH IS EUDAMONIA?

WHICH IS EVOLVE?

WHICH IS EXALTING?

WHICH IS EXSTATISFY?

WHICH IS EXULTANT?

WHICH IS ASTRONOMICAL?

WHICH IS CHAMPION?

WHICH IS CHAMP?

WHICH IS ELECTRIC?

WHICH IS ENORMOUS?

WHICH IS EXCEPTIONAL?

WHICH IS EXCITING?

WHICH IS EXQUISITE?

WHICH IS EFFORTLESSNESS?

WHICH IS EUNOIA?

WHICH IS ECOSOPHY?

WHICH EBULLIENCE?

WHICH IS EMBRACE?

WHICH IS EMPOWERING WORDS?

WHICH IS ENCOURAGING WORDS?

WHICH IS ERLEBNIS?

WHICH IS EFFORTLESS EASE EFFORTLESSLY?

WHICH IS EKAGGATA?

WHICH IS EMBODY THE LOVE?

WHICH IS EARTHING?

WHICH IS EVER-JOYOUS?

WHICH IS EVER-JOYOUS NOW?

WHICH IS ETHEREAL?

WHICH IS ENDLESS?

WHICH IS E MA HO?

WHICH IS FANTASTIC?

WHICH IS FEEL GOOD?

WHICH IS FEELING GOOD?

WHICH IS FLOW?

WHICH IS FLOWING?

WHICH IS FABULOUS?

WHICH IS FAIR?

WHICH IS FAITH?

WHICH IS FAITHFUL?

WHICH IS FAME?

WHICH IS FAVORITE?

WHICH IS FAIRNESS?

WHICH IS FAMILY?

WHICH IS FIDELITY?

WHICH IS FLEXIBILITY?

WHICH IS FOCUS?

WHICH IS FLOURISH?

WHICH IS FORGIVE?

WHICH IS FORGIVING?

WHICH IS FORGIVENESS?

WHICH IS FORTITUDE?

WHICH IS FREE?

WHICH IS FREEDOM?

WHICH IS FRUGALITY?

WHICH IS FUN?

WHICH IS FUTURE?

WHICH IS FRIEND?

WHICH IS FRIENDLY?

WHICH IS FRIENDSHIP?

WHICH IS FRIENDLINESS?

WHICH IS FASCINATE?

WHICH IS FASCINATED?

WHICH IS FULFILL?

WHICH IS FULFILLED?

WHICH IS FOOD?

WHICH IS FEISTY?

WHICH IS FEISTINESS?

WHICH IS FEASIBLE?

WHICH IS FINE?

WHICH IS FEARLESS?

WHICH IS FESTIVE?

WHICH IS FESTIVENESS?

WHICH IS FIT?

WHICH IS FANTABULOUS?

WHICH IS FREECYCLE?

WHICH IS FUNERIFIC?

WHICH IS FUNOLOGY?

WHICH IS FLAWLESS?

WHICH IS FAMOUS?

WHICH IS FANCY?

WHICH IS FLASHY?

WHICH IS FTW?

WHICH IS FUNNY JOKES?

WHICH IS FLAUNTING?

WHICH IS FONDLE?

WHICH IS FRIC-TIONLESSLY?

WHICH IS FLAWLESSLY?

WHICH IS FLOURISHING?

WHICH IS FORTUITOUS?

WHICH IS FUN-LOVING?

WHICH IS FREE-SPIRITED?

WHICH IS FELICITY?

WHICH IS GLOW?

WHICH IS GENEROUS?

WHICH IS GENEROSITY?

WHICH IS GENERATE?

WHICH IS GENIAL?

WHICH IS GENIUS?

WHICH IS GENUINE?

WHICH IS GIFT?

WHICH IS GIVE?

WHICH IS GIVING?

WHICH IS GOOD?

WHICH IS GOODNESS?

WHICH IS GOING THE EXTRA MILE?

WHICH IS GRACE?

WHICH IS GRATITUDE?

WHICH IS GRATEFULNESS?

WHICH IS GROW?

WHICH IS GROWTH?

WHICH IS GUIDE?

WHICH IS GUIDING?

WHICH IS GUIDANCE?

WHICH IS GOD?

WHICH IS GROUNDED?

WHICH IS GLORY?

WHICH IS GODLINESS?

WHICH IS GOOD-FEELING?

WHICH IS GROOVY?

WHICH IS GIDDY?

WHICH IS GLAD?

WHICH IS GOOD HEALTH?

WHICH IS GLAMOR?

WHICH IS GIGGLING?

WHICH IS GODDESS?

WHICH IS GORGEOUS?

WHICH IS GORGEOUSNESS?

WHICH IS GRANDIOSITY?

WHICH IS GENERAVITY?

WHICH IS GENTLEMAN?

WHICH IS GARGANTUAN?

WHICH IS GRAND?

WHICH IS GREAT?

WHICH IS GINGER?

WHICH IS GOOD-HUMORED?

WHICH IS GOODWILL?

WHICH IS GREATFUL?

WHICH IS GEMUTLICHKEIT?

WHICH IS GIBIGIANA?

WHICH IS GIGIL?

WHICH IS GOOD INDWELLING SPIRIT?

WHICH IS GOOD WORD?

WHICH IS GOOD WORDS?

WHICH IS GOOD-HUMORED?

WHICH IS GOODWILL?

WHICH IS GOOD FORTUNE?

WHICH IS GYPSY SOUL?

WHICH IS GAME-CHANGER?

WHICH IS GENERATOR OF LIFE?

WHICH IS GRACEFULLY?

WHICH IS GRACIOUSNESS?

WHICH IS GOLDILOCKS?

WHICH IS GENUINENESS?

WHICH IS GREAT ZEAL?

WHICH IS GOOD DONE IN SECRET?

WHICH IS HOPE?

WHICH IS HOPEFULNESS?

WHICH IS HAPPINESS?

WHICH IS HAPPY?

WHICH IS HAPPILY?

WHICH IS HARMONIOUS?

WHICH IS HARMONIZE?

WHICH IS HARMONY?

WHICH IS HEALTH?

WHICH IS HEALTHY?

WHICH IS HEART?

WHICH IS HELLO?

WHICH IS HELP?

WHICH IS HELPFUL?

WHICH IS HELPING?

WHICH IS HOT?

WHICH IS HONEST?

WHICH IS HONESTY?

WHICH IS HUMAN?

WHICH IS HUMOR?

WHICH IS HELPFULNESS?

WHICH IS HERO?

WHICH IS HEROISM?

WHICH IS HOLY?

WHICH IS HOLINESS?

WHICH IS HONOR?

WHICH IS HOSPITALITY?

WHICH IS HUMBLE?

WHICH IS HEAVEN?

WHICH IS HEAVENLY?

WHICH IS HALO?

WHICH IS HEARTFELT?

WHICH IS HEARTWARMING?

WHICH IS ONE-POINTEDNESS?

WHICH IS HAPPY HEARTED?

WHICH IS HEEDFUL?

WHICH IS HANDSOME?

WHICH IS HUGE?

WHICH IS HIGH-SPIRITEDNESS?

WHICH IS HIGHLY DISTINGUISHED?

WHICH IS HAPPY WORDS?

WHICH IS HEART-OPENING?

WHICH IS HOSPITABLE?

WHICH IS HUMAN FLOURISHING?

WHICH IS HIGHLY DISTINGUISHED?

WHICH IS HARNESS?

WHICH IS HEIGHTENED?

WHICH IS HOLISTIC?

WHICH IS HOLY SPIRIT?

WHICH IS HALL OF AWESOMENESS?

WHICH IS HONEY BADGER?

WHICH IS HIGHER CONSCIOUSNESS?

WHICH IS HALYCON?

WHICH IS HABITUATION?

WHICH IS HAKUNA MATATA?

WHICH IS IMAGINATION?

WHICH IS INSPIRE?

WHICH IS INSPIRATION?

WHICH IS INSPIRED?

WHICH IS INSPIRATIONAL?

WHICH IS IN-LOVE?

WHICH IS IDEA?

WHICH IS INCREDIBLE?

WHICH IS INNOVATE?

WHICH IS INNOVATION?

WHICH IS INTERESTING?

WHICH IS INTEREST?

WHICH IS INTERESTED?

WHICH IS IMPROVEMENT?

WHICH IS INDEPENDENCE?

WHICH IS INFLUENCE?

WHICH IS INGENUITY?

WHICH IS INNER PEACE?

WHICH IS INSIGHT?

WHICH IS INSIGHTFULNESS?

WHICH IS INSIGHTFUL?

WHICH IS INTEGRITY?

WHICH IS INTELLIGENCE?

WHICH IS INTELLIGENT?

WHICH IS INTENSITY?

WHICH IS INTIMACY?

WHICH IS INTUITIVENESS?

WHICH IS INVENTIVENESS?

WHICH IS INVESTING?

WHICH IS INTENTION?

WHICH IS INVIGORATE?

WHICH IS INVIGORATED?

WHICH IS INTRIGUED?

WHICH IS INVOLVE?

WHICH IS INVOLVED?

WHICH IS INCLUSION?

WHICH IS INNOCENT?

WHICH IS INEFFABLE?

WHICH IS INEFFABILITY?

WHICH IS INTREPID?

WHICH IS IDEALISM?

WHICH IS ILLUMINATION?

WHICH IS ILLUMINATED?

WHICH IS INCOMPARABLE?

WHICH IS INVINCIBLE?

WHICH IS INQUISITIVE?

WHICH IS INFINITE?

WHICH IS INFINITY?

WHICH IS ILLUSTRIOUS?

WHICH IS INNER?

WHICH IS ICHARIBA CHODE?

WHICH IS IKIGAI?

WHICH IS INCREDIBLE CUTENESS?

WHICH IS INDWELLING?

WHICH IS INSPIRATIONAL WORDS?

WHICH IS INSPIRING WORD?

WHICH IS INSPIRING WORDS?

WHICH IS IRIDESCENT?

WHICH IS ILLUSTRIOUS?

WHICH IS INNER?

WHICH IS INNER SPIRIT?

WHICH IS INTERCONNECTED?

WHICH IS INTERCONNECTIVITY?

WHICH IS INTUITION?

WHICH IS INCLUSIVENESS?

WHICH IS JOY?

WHICH IS JOYFUL?

WHICH IS JOYOUS?

WHICH IS JOKE?

WHICH IS JOLLY?

WHICH IS JOVIAL?

WHICH IS JUST?

WHICH IS JUSTICE?

WHICH IS JUBILANT?

WHICH IS JUVENESCENT?

WHICH IS JUMPY?

WHICH IS JAMMIN?

WHICH IS JUBILINGO?

WHICH IS KINDNESS?

WHICH IS KIND?

WHICH IS KIND-HEART?

WHICH IS KINDLY?

WHICH IS KEEP-UP?

WHICH IS KISS?

WHICH IS KNOWLEDGE?

WHICH IS KITTENS?

WHICH IS KEEN?

WHICH IS KAAJHUAB?

WHICH IS KALON?

WHICH IS KILIG?

WHICH IS KIND WORDS?

WHICH IS KOIBITO KIBUN?

WHICH IS WHICH IS KI?

WHICH IS KALEIDOSCOPES OF BUTTERFLIES?

WHICH IS LIKE?

WHICH IS LAUGH?

WHICH IS LAUGHING?

WHICH IS LEARN?

WHICH IS WHICH IS LEARNING?

WHICH IS LIFE, WHICH IS LIVE?

WHICH IS LIVING?

WHICH IS LUXURY?

WHICH IS LONGEVITY?

WHICH IS LOYALTY?

WHICH IS LOYAL?

WHICH IS LOVE?

WHICH IS LOVABLE?

WHICH IS LOVING?

WHICH IS LIBERTY?

WHICH IS LOGIC?

WHICH IS LEADER?

WHICH IS LEADERSHIP?

WHICH IS LUCK?

WHICH IS LUCKY?

WHICH IS LIGHT?

WHICH IS LOVING-KINDNESS?

WHICH IS WHICH IS LIVELY?

WHICH IS LIFE OF THE PARTY?

WHICH IS LOVELY?

WHICH IS LOVING ACCEPTANCE?

WHICH IS LOVING FEELINGS?

WHICH IS LIGHTWORKER?

WHICH IS LEADING?

WHICH IS LIGHT FOG?

WHICH IS LIVES THROUGH?

WHICH IS LOVE WORDS?

WHICH IS LOVER OF BEAUTY?

WHICH IS LUSTROUS?

WHICH IS LUSTROUS COLORS?

LIGHT-HEARTED?

WHICH IS LEEWAY?

WHICH IS LET GO?

WHICH IS LETTING GO?

WHICH IS LIVELINESS?

WHICH IS LOVE FULFILLED?

WHICH IS LOVING ATTENTION?

WHICH IS MEANING?

WHICH IS MEANINGFUL?

WHICH IS MORE?

WHICH IS MAGNIFICENT?

WHICH IS MAJESTY?

WHICH IS MANY?

WHICH IS MARVELOUS?

WHICH IS MERIT?

WHIS IS MOTIVATE?

WHICH IS MIRACLE?

WHICH IS MAGIC?

WHICH IS MAKING A DIFFERENCE?

WHICH IS MASTERY?

WHICH IS MATURITY?

WHICH IS MINDFUL?

WHICH IS MINDFULNESS?

WHICH IS MODESTY?

WHICH IS MOTIVATION?

WHICH IS MOTIVATIONAL?

WHICH IS MERCY?

WHICH IS MEDITATION?

WHICH IS MIND-BLOWING?

WHICH IS MELLOW?

WHICH IS MOVED?

WHICH IS MOVEMENT?

WHICH IS MUTUALITY?

WHICH IS MOURNING?

MELIORISM?

WHICH IS MENCH?

WHICH IS MINDSIGHT?

WHICH IS MINDSIGHT?

WHICH IS MAJOR?

WHICH IS MILD?

WHICH IS MEANINGFUL WORDS?

WHICH IS MEMORABLE?

WHICH IS MORPHING?

WHICH IS MOTIVATED WORDS?

WHICH IS MOTIVATING WORDS?

WHICH IS MOTIVATIONAL WORDS?

WHICH IS MOVING?

WHICH IS MAGNETIC TO LOVE?

WHICH IS MIRTHFUL?

WHICH IS MYRIAD?

WHICH IS MOJO?

WHICH IS NOBLE?

WHICH IS NURTURING?

WHICH IS NURTURE?

WHICH IS NON-RESISTANCE?

WHICH IS NON-RESISTANT?

WHICH IS NEW?

WHICH IS NICE?

WHICH IS NIRVANA?

WHICH IS NEAT?

WHICH IS NATURE-MADE?

WHICH IS NOURISH?

WHICH IS NOURISHED?

WHICH IS NOURISHING?

WHICH IS NOURISHMENT?

WHICH IS NAMASTE?

WHICH IS NEOTENY?

WHICH IS NICE WORDS?

WHICH IS NOVATURIENT?

WHICH IS NON-DUALITY?

WHICH IS OPTIMIST?

WHICH IS OPTIMISTIC?

WHICH IS OUTSTANDING?

WHICH IS OK?

WHICH IS ON?

WHICH IS ONWARDS?

WHICH IS OPEN?

WHICH IS OPENLY?

WHICH IS OPENING?

WHICH IS OPEN-MINDED?

WHICH IS OPPORTUNITY?

WHICH IS ORIGINAL?

WHICH IS OPENNESS?

WHICH IS OPTIMISM?

WHICH IS ORDER?

WHICH IS ORGANIZATION?

WHICH IS ORIGINALITY?

WHICH IS OUTCOME?

WHICH IS ORIENTATION?

WHICH IS OBEDIENT?

WHICH IS OPEN HEARTED?

WHICH IS OMG?

WHICH IS OVERCOME?

WHICH IS OM MANI PADME HUM?

WHICH IS OUTGOING?

WHICH IS ONENESS?

WHICH IS OUTERNATIONALIST?

WHICH IS OVERLY OPTIMISTIC?

WHICH IS ORENDA?

WHICH IS OWNING YOUR POWER?

WHICH IS ONEUP?

WHICH IS OMNISCIENCE?

WHICH IS OKAGE SAMA?

WHICH IS PERFECT?

WHICH IS PERFECTION?

WHICH IS POSITIVE ENERGY?

WHICH IS POSITIVE THOUGHTS?

WHICH IS POSITIVE EVENTS?

WHICH IS POSITIVE CIRCUMSTANCES?

WHICH IS POSITIVE BELIEFS?

WHICH IS PEACE?

WHICH IS PACIFY?

WHICH IS PARADISE?

WHICH IS PARADISIAC?

WHICH IS PASSION?

WHICH IS PASSIONATE?

WHICH IS PLEASE?

WHICH IS PURE?

WHICH IS PERCEPTIVENESS?

WHICH IS PERSEVERANCE?

WHICH IS PERSISTENCE?

WHICH IS PERSONAL GROWTH?

WHICH IS PLEASURE?

WHICH IS POSITIVE ATTITUDE?

WHICH IS POSITIVE WORDS?

WHICH IS POWER?

WHICH IS POWERFUL?

WHICH IS PRACTICALITY?

WHICH IS PRECISION?

WHICH IS PREPAREDNESS?

WHICH IS PRESENCE?

WHICH IS PRESERVATION?

WHICH IS PRIVACY?

WHICH IS PROACTIVITY?

WHICH IS PROACTIVE?

WHICH IS PROGRESS?

WHICH IS PROSPERITY PROSPEROUS?

WHICH IS PUNCTUALITY?

WHICH IS PUNCTUAL?

WHICH IS PATIENCE?

WHICH IS PROUD?

WHICH IS PLEASED?

WHICH IS PLAY?

WHICH IS PLAYFUL?

WHICH IS PLAYFULNESS?

WHICH IS PARTICIPATION?

WHICH IS PURPOSE?

WHICH IS PICK-ME-UP?

WHICH IS PRONIA?

WHICH IS PIOUS?

WHICH IS PUPPIES?

WHICH IS POLITE?

WHICH IS POSITIVE MIND?

WHICH IS POSITIVE THINKING?

WHICH IS PRETTY?

WHICH IS PRECIOUS?

WHICH IS PARDON?

WHICH IS PERKINESS?

WHICH IS PIQUANCY?

WHICH IS POSICHOICE?

WHICH IS POSIDRIVING?

WHICH IS POSIFIT?

WHICH IS POSILENZ?

WHICH IS POSIMASS?

WHICH IS POSIMINDER?

WHICH IS POSIRATIO?

WHICH IS POSIRIPPLE?

WHICH IS POSIRIPPLER?

WHICH IS POSIRIPPLES?

WHICH IS POSISINGER?

WHICH IS POSISITE?

WHICH IS POSISTRENGTH?

WHICH IS POSITIBILITARIAN?

WHICH IS POSITRACTION?

WHICH IS POSITUDE?

WHICH IS POSIVALUES?

WHICH IS POSIWORD?

WHICH IS POSSIBILITARIAN?

WHICH IS PROMPTNESS?

WHICH IS PROTO?

WHICH IS PRICELESS?

WHICH IS PEP?

WHICH IS PEPPINESS?

WHICH IS PERMALICIOUS?

WHICH IS PLUCKY?

WHICH IS POLLYANNAISM?

WHICH IS PRIDE?

WHICH IS POSITIVE FEELINGS?

WHICH IS PEACE OF MIND?

WHICH IS PEACEFUL WORDS?

WHICH IS PETRICHOR?

WHICH IS PHILOCALIST?

WHICH IS POSITIVE EMOTIONS?

WHICH IS POSITIVE FEELINGS?

WHICH IS POSITIVE VOCABULARY?

WHICH IS POWER WORDS?

WHICH IS POWERFUL POSITIVE WORDS?

WHICH IS POWERFUL WORDS?

WHICH IS POWER-ON?

WHICH IS POWER-UP?

WHICH PROTECT?

WHICH IS POLITENESS?

WHICH IS POUR YOUR LOVE?

WHICH IS POWERFUL POSSIBILITY?

WHICH IS PRIVILEGE?

WHICH IS PROPITIOUS?

WHICH IS POSITIVE THESAURUS?

WHICH IS POSITIVE ADJECTIVES?

WHICH IS PICTURESQUE?

WHICH IS PRANA?

WHICH IS PANACHE?

WHICH IS QUALITY?

WHICH IS QUIET?

WHICH IS QUIETNESS?

WHICH IS QUAINT?

WHICH IS QUIESCENT?

WHICH IS QUEENLY?

WHICH IS QUICKENING?

WHICH IS QUIDDITY?

WHICH IS QUIESCENT MIND?

WHICH IS QUALITY WORDS?

WHICH IS QUANTUMNESS?

WHICH IS QUANTUM CONSCIOUSNESS?

WHICH IS RESPECT?

WHICH IS RADIANT?

WHICH IS READY?

WHICH IS READINESS?

WHICH IS REAL?

WHICH IS REALITY?

WHICH IS REASON?

WHICH IS RECOMMEND?

WHICH IS REFRESH?

WHICH IS REFRESHED?

WHICH IS RELAX?

WHICH IS RELAXED?

WHICH IS RELIEF?

WHICH IS RELIEVE?

WHICH IS RELIEVED?

WHICH IS REMARKABLE?

WHICH IS RATIONALITY?

WHICH IS RECOGNITION?

WHICH IS RELATIONSHIPS?

WHICH IS RELIABLE?

WHICH IS RELIABILITY?

WHICH IS RELIGION?

WHICH IS RESOURCEFULNESS?

WHICH IS RESPONSIBILITY?

WHICH IS RIGHTEOUSNESS?

WHICH IS RISK-TAKING?

WHICH IS ROMANCE?

WHICH IS REVELATION?

WHICH IS REVIVED?

WHICH IS RESTORE?

WHICH IS RESTORED?

WHICH IS REST?

WHICH IS RESTED?

WHICH IS RENEW?

WHICH IS RENEWED?

WHICH IS REJUVENATE?

WHICH IS REJUVENATED?

WHICH IS RAPTURE?

WHICH IS RAPTUROUS?

WHICH IS RESILIENT?

WHICH IS RESILIENCE?

WHICH IS REVERENCE?

WHICH IS RIPE?

WHICH IS REBORN?

WHICH IS RELATEDNESS?

WHICH IS RASASVADA?

WHICH IS REPOSE?

WHICH IS ROSINESS?

WHICH IS RELENT?

WHICH IS RENOWNED?

WHICH IS RESPECTED?

WHICH IS RAINBOW?

WHICH IS ROMANTIC?

WHICH IS RELENT?

WHICH IS RENOWNED?

WHICH IS RADIATE?

WHICH IS RECOGNIZE?

WHICH IS WHICH IS RELEASING?

WHICH IS RIGHTFUL?

WHICH IS ROCKSTAR?

WHICH IS SCOPE?

WHICH IS SMILE?

WHICH IS SMILING?

WHICH IS SOULMATE?

WHICH IS SOUL?

WHICH IS SOULFUL?

WHICH IS SACRED?

WHICH IS SAFE?

WHICH IS SAFETY?

WHICH IS SECURE?

WHICH IS SECURED?

WHICH IS SECURITY?

WHICH IS SUSTAIN?

WHICH IS SUSTAINED?

WHICH IS SAVE?

WHICH IS SAVINGS?

WHICH IS SIMPLE?

WHICH IS SIMPLIFY?

WHICH IS SELFLESSNESS?

WHICH IS SELF-ESTEEM?

WHICH IS SERVICE?

WHICH IS SIMPLICITY?

WHICH IS SINCERITY?

WHICH IS SKILL?

WHICH IS SKILLED?

WHICH IS SPIRIT?

WHICH IS SERENE ?

WHICH IS SERENITY?

WHICH IS STABILITY?

WHICH IS STRENGTH ?

WHICH IS STYLE?

WHICH IS SYSTEMATIZATION?

WHICH IS SELF-LOVE?

WHICH IS STRIVE?

WHICH IS SALVATION?

WHICH IS SELF- RESPECT?

WHICH IS SELF-FORGIVENESS?

WHICH IS SERVE?

WHICH IS SYMPATHETIC?

WHICH IS SELF-COMPASSION?

WHICH IS SELF-KINDNESS?

WHICH IS SPELLBOUND?

WHICH IS STIMULATED?

WHICH IS STIMULATING?

WHICH IS STIMULATION?

WHICH IS SATISFIED?

WHICH IS STILL?

WHICH IS SURPRISED?

WHICH IS SLEEP?

WHICH IS SEXUAL EXPRESSION?

WHICH IS SHELTER?

WHICH IS SELF-EXPRESSION?

WHICH IS SPACE?

WHICH IS SPACIOUS?

WHICH IS SPONTANEITY?

WHICH IS SPONTANEOUS?

WHICH IS SUNSHINE?

WHICH IS SPARK?

WHICH IS SPARKLE?

WHICH IS SPARKLES?

WHICH IS SWEET?

WHICH IS SWEETNESS?

WHICH IS SUPPORT?

WHICH IS SUPPORTING?

WHICH IS SUPPORTED?

WHICH IS SEXY?

WHICH IS SEXINESS?

WHICH IS SUPREME?

WHICH IS SUCCULENT?

WHICH IS SWEETHEART?

WHICH IS STUDY?

WHICH IS STUDIOUS?

WHICH IS SAVOUR?

WHICH IS SAVOURING?

WHICH IS SUFFICIENT?

WHICH IS STUPENDOUS?

WHICH IS SWAG?

WHICH IS SWAGGY?

WHICH IS SPLENDID?

WHICH IS SMART?

WHICH IS SPECTACULAR?

WHICH IS SPECIAL?

WHICH IS SERENDIPITY?

WHICH IS SYNERGY?

WHICH IS SHINE?

WHICH IS SHINING?

WHICH IS START?

WHICH IS STEADFASTNESS?

WHICH IS SUBLIME?

WHICH IS SUNNINESS?

WHICH IS SUPERPOWER?

WHICH IS SPUNKY?

WHICH IS SHAPE-SHIFTING VIRTUOSO?

WHICH IS SOUL-STRETCHING?

WHICH IS STRONG WORDS?

WHICH IS SACRED SPACE?

WHICH IS SHIFT IN FOCUS?

WHICH IS SHOW UP MORE PRESENT?

WHICH IS STELLAR?

WHICH IS SUPERCHARGE?

WHICH IS SUPERCHARGED?

WHICH IS SYMPTOMS OF GREATNESS?

WHICH IS SYNCHRONICITY?

WHICH IS SASSY?

WHICH IS SUPERCALIFRAGILISTIC?

WHICH IS SUPERCALIFRAGILISTICEXPIALIDOCIOUS?

WHICH IS SLAYING YOUR DRAGON?

WHICH IS TRUE?

WHICH IS TRUST?

WHICH IS TRUSTING?

WHICH IS TACT?

WHICH IS TEACH?

WHICH IS TEACHABLE?

WHICH IS TEAM?

WHICH IS THANKFUL?

WHICH IS THANK?

WHICH IS THANK-YOU?

WHICH IS THANKFULNESS?

WHICH IS THERAPY?

WHICH IS TIME?

WHICH IS TEAMWORK?

WHICH IS TIMELINESS?

WHICH IS TOLERANCE?

WHICH IS TRADITION?

WHICH IS TRANQUIL?

WHICH IS TRANQUILITY?

WHICH IS TRUTH?

WHICH IS TRUTHFULNESS?

WHICH IS TENDER?

WHICH IS THRILLED?

WHICH IS TOUCH?

WHICH IS TOUCHED?

WHICH IS TICKLED?

WHICH IS TO MATTER?

WHICH IS TO KNOW?

WHICH IS TO BE KNOWN?

WHICH IS TO BE SEEN?

WHICH IS TRANSFORMATIVE?

WHICH IS TRANSFORMATION?

WHICH IS TRANSFORM?

WHICH IS TRIUMPH?

WHICH IS THRIVE?

WHICH IS THRIVING?

WHICH IS TENACITY?

WHICH IS TO BE?

WHICH IS TRANSPARENT?

WHICH IS TEMUL?

WHICH IS TENDERLY?

WHICH IS TIDSOPTIMIST?

WHICH IS TIME OPTIMIST?

WHICH IS TO LET GO?

WHICH IS THE GREAT SPIRIT?

UNIFICATION?

WHICH IS UNIQUE?

WHICH IS UPLIFT?

WHICH IS ULTIMATE?

WHICH IS UNCONDITIONAL?

WHICH IS UPGRADE?

WHICH IS USEFUL?

WHICH IS USER-FRIENDLY?

WHICH IS UNITY?

WHICH IS UNDERSTAND?

WHICH IS UNDERSTANDING?

WHICH IS UNDERSTOOD?

WHICH IS UNIFICATION OF MIND?

WHICH IS UP?

WHICH IS UPSKILL?

WHICH IS UNBELIEVABLE?

WHICH IS UNFLAPPABLE?

WHICH IS UNREAL?

WHICH IS UTTER AMAZEMENT?

WHICH IS UNABASHED?

WHICH IS UNABASHED PLEASURE?

WHICH IS UNBEARABLY CUTE?

WHICH IS UNHURRY?

WHICH IS UNBELIEVABLE?

UNFLAPPABLE?

WHICH IS UNREAL?

WHICH IS UTTER AMAZEMENT?

WHICH IS UP-LEVELED?

WHICH IS VITALITY?

WHICH IS VALUE?

WHICH IS VALUES?

WHICH IS VALUABLE?

WHICH IS VIRTUOUS?

WHICH IS VALID?

WHICH IS VERIFY?

WHICH IS VERY?

WHICH IS VIABLE?

WHICH IS VIRTUE?

WHICH IS VICTORY?

WHICH IS VICTORIOUS?

WHICH IS VARIETY?

WHICH IS VULNERABILITY?

WHICH IS VULNERABLE?

WHICH IS VIBRANT?

WHICH IS VOW?

WHICH IS VIM?

WHICH IS VIGOR?

WHICH IS VENERATION?

WHICH IS VOCABULEVERAGE?

WHICH IS VERSATILITY?

WHICH IS UBUNTU?

WHICH IS WORTH?

WHICH IS WORTHY?

WHICH IS WORTHINESS?

WHICH IS WEALTH?

WHICH IS WARM?

WHICH IS WARMTH?

WHICH IS WELCOME?

WHICH IS WILL?

WHICH IS WILLING?

WHICH IS WILLINGNESS?

WHICH IS WISDOM?

WHICH IS WISE?

WHICH IS WON?

WHICH IS WONDERFUL?

WHICH IS WELL-BEING?

WHICH IS WHOLEHEARTEDNESS?

WHICH IS WOW?

WHICH IS WONDER?

WHICH IS WATER?

WHICH IS WELL?

WHICH IS WELLNESS?

WHICH IS WELFARE?

WHICH IS WHOLE?

WHICH IS WONDER?

WHICH IS WORKING?

WHICH IS WIN?

WHICH IS WINNABLE?

WHICH IS WINNING?

WHICH IS WALWALUN?

WHICH IS WEB OF RELATEDNESS?

WHICH IS WHOLEHEARTEDLY?

WHICH IS WILLING TO LEARN?

WHICH IS WONDROUS?

WHICH IS WORLD-BUILDER?

WHICH IS WORTHINESS TO TAKE UP SPACE?

WHICH IS WANDERLUST?

WHICH IS XO?

WHICH IS X-RAY VISION?

WHICH IS XENODOCHIAL?

WHICH IS XFACTOR?

WHICH IS XENOPHILE?

WHICH IS XENIAL?

WHICH IS YES?

WHICH IS YOUTH?

WHICH IS YOUTHFUL?

WHICH IS YOUNG?

WHICH IS YOUNG?

WHICH IS AT-HEART?

WHICH IS YIPPEE?

WHICH IS YAY?

WHICH IS YEARN?

WHICH IS YEA?

WHICH IS YEAH?

WHICH IS YUMMY?

WHICH IS YEN?

WHICH IS YESABILITY?

WHICH IS YUGEN?

WHICH IS YARAANA?

WHICH IS YESABLE?

WHICH IS YOU ARE LOVED?

WHICH IS YOUR TRUE VALUE?

WHICH IS ZEALOUS?

WHICH IS ZEAL?

WHICH IS ZEST?

WHICH IS ZESTY?

WHICH IS ZESTFUL?

WHICH IS ZIPPY?

WHICH IS ZING?

WHICH IS ZAPPY?

WHICH IS ZANY?

WHICH IS ZEST FOR LIFE?

WHICH IS ZAJEBISCIE?